THE BACKSIDE
OF CALVARY

. . . Where Healing Stained the Cross

THE BACKSIDE OF CALVARY

. . . Where Healing Stained the Cross

by
Rod Parsley

Harrison House
Tulsa, Oklahoma

Unless otherwise indicated, all Scripture quotations are taken from the *King James Version* of the Bible.

The Backside of Calvary
. . . Where Healing Stained the Cross
(Formerly ISBN 1-880244-01-2)
ISBN 0-89274-897-4
Copyright © 1991 by Rod Parsley
World Harvest Church
P. O. Box 32932
Columbus, Ohio 43232

Published by Harrison House, Inc.
P. O. Box 35035
Tulsa, Oklahoma 74153

DEDICATION

To my sister, Debbie Parsley King.

When I think of God's healing power, you are the first example that comes to mind. From the car accident that almost took your life, on through the months of recovery that followed, your quiet strength and unshakable faith was -- and remains -- living proof that healing is not a fable, but fact.

CONTENTS

FOREWORD

In our desperate, imperfect world, its assistance is critical. The need for this valuable commodity spans every social, economic, racial and age barrier. Everyone, at some point in their life, is faced with the urgency of choosing whether or not to believe in the existence of... healing.

The majority of the books I have read on this topic usually deal more with ''how to build your *faith*'' rather than exploring the actual ingredients of healing itself. This book breaks the mold and gives you the background necessary to better comprehend the reasons behind healing, thereby making it *easier* to understand and believe.

What event made healing necessary? When did this terrible incident take place? How did mankind figure in? What role did God play in this drama? How did He remedy the situation? Where does healing fit into God's salvation plan? Who is eligible to receive it?

All of these questions can be answered by simply pointing to one place, one incident, one moment in time. Suffice it to say that everything is made clear on *the Backside of Calvary*.

Rod Parsley
Columbus, Ohio

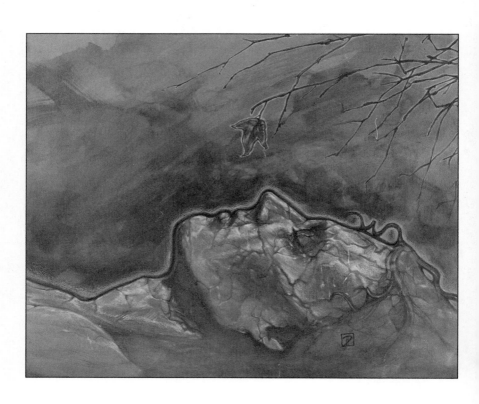

"The Creator Himself knelt on the
muddy banks of earth's freshly formed
shore and carved out a figure in
His Own image. It was the
shape of a man."

PARADISE
QUARANTINED

"..One single exposure to Satan was all that
was needed to transmit the communicable
disease of sin into the bloodline of all
humanity."

CHAPTER

I

We live in a temporal, imperfect world. Nothing in this physical environment goes unscarred by the weathering hands of time. Flowers wither, rocks crumble, iron rusts, and even our fragile human bodies slowly, but surely, deteriorate. Everything about this physical sphere is in a state of decay, nevertheless, our world was not created with this affliction. The disease was contracted.

In the beginning, God spoke, and out of the void of space something marvelous was created -- Life! With just a word, He invented the sun for the day shift and put the moon and stars on night duty. By His spoken thought, rivers began to flow and mountains rose to the sky. On and above earth's greening landscape, He scattered a diversity of living things. And along the shore, He ordered the seven seas to their respective boundaries.

...And God said, 'Let there be light'...And God said, 'Let there be firmament'...And God said, 'Let the waters under the heavens be gathered together in one place'...And God said, 'Let the waters bring forth swarms of living creatures, and let birds fly above the earth across the firmament of the heavens'.

(Gen.1:3,6,9,20 RSV)

Yet though He had created a vast, global menagerie, God discovered that there was no one in the world for Him to talk to. In those early moments of time, the Lord realized that He desired someone with whom He could commune, fellowship. Therefore, the Creator Himself knelt on the muddy banks of Earth's freshly formed shore and lovingly carved out a figure in His Own image. It was the shape of a man.

...And God said, Let us make man in our image, after our likeness...And the Lord God formed man of the dust of the ground, and breathed into his nostrils the breath of life; and man became a living soul.

(Genesis 1:26, 2:7)

God *made* a man. He did not speak humanity into existence, as He had with the stars, the earth and all other living things. When it came to the creation of His special companion, God took an unusual interest and "physically" involved Himself in the process.

By the Creator's hands-on approach, it is obvious that the Lord desired a unique relationship with man. And what a extraordinary creation he was!

The moment God's divine breath entered man, he became superior to all other forms of earthly life. Not only was Adam's complex physical structure a work of divine craftsmanship, he was capable of such feats as abstract thought, original concepts and the all-important attribute of free will.

Man was a one-of-a-kind combination of flesh and spirit, a creation that could actually have fellowship with the Almighty! Within him, the Lord placed the mind and emotions of a soul and the priceless gift of an eternal spirit. And the Creator housed this rare combination in a clay "earthsuit" called the body.

After six busy days of creating, God stepped back and surveyed the length and breadth of His handiwork. Seeing that it was good, He gave Adam and Eve, the first man and woman, total dominion over it all.

MUTINY IN THE MIDST OF BOUNTY

It was a world of perfection, a garden paradise where the concepts of need, worry and pain were unknown. Abundance was commonplace. And daily conversations with God were as natural and ordinary as the breeze that rustled through the fruit-filled trees.

Man had been granted control of all that he surveyed -- that is except for one small patch of ground.

And the Lord God commanded the man, saying, Of every tree of the garden thou mayest freely eat: But of the tree of the knowledge of good and evil, thou shalt not eat of it: for in the day that thou eatest thereof thou shalt surely die.

(Genesis 2:16,17)

It seems reasonable that if Adam could be faithful with the ''little things'' of this world, in time, humanity would be ''made rulers over many'' worlds throughout the Creator's vast domain.

But Satan slithered into the picture.

Enraged by God's fellowship with man and covetous of the world which the Lord had graciously given to His creation, the devil set his sights on paradise.

Why was Satan so opposed to the new world and its inhabitants? In actuality, humanity and its surroundings meant very little to him. The devil's motivation was not to *get to man* necessarily, but rather, to *get back at God*. Satan wanted revenge.

Once before, Lucifer had tried to gain control of God's property. Supposing himself to be ''like the most High'', Satan attempted a Heavenly coup. The prophet Isaiah recounts the story this way:

...How art thou fallen from heaven, O Lucifer, son of the morning! How art thou cut down to the ground, which didst weaken the nations! For thou hast said

in thine heart, I will ascend into heaven,
I will exalt my throne above the stars of
God: I will sit also upon the mount of the
congregation, in the sides of the north. I
will ascend above the heights of the
clouds; I will be like the most High. Yet
thou shalt be brought down to hell, to the
sides of the pit.
(Isaiah 14: 12-15)

Satan's selfish scheme backfired, and he, along with his deceived followers, were banished for eternity. The New Testament concludes the episode with the postscript:

And he (Jesus) said unto them, I
beheld Satan as lightning fall from heaven.
(Luke 10:18)

Having been summarily booted out of Glory, it is safe to presume that Satan was on the lookout for a chance to strike back. And upon seeing how pleased God was with His "new" creation, the devil found a fresh target.

This time, however, Lucifer did not voice his intentions aloud. He approached his objective under the subtle guise of a serpent. And using the same infectious words he had used to woo a third of heaven's angels into hell (Rev. 12:4), the serpent struck back and sank his venomous fangs into the bloodstream of humanity.

SELFISHNESS: REACHING FOR THE TREE

Slipping into the Garden, the devil approached Eve and slyly drew her attention to the one and only restriction God had imposed:

...And he said unto the woman, Yea, hath God said, Ye shall not eat of every tree of the garden? And the woman said unto the serpent, We may eat of the fruit of the trees of the garden: But of the fruit of the tree which is in the midst of the garden, God hath said, Ye shall not eat of it, neither shall ye touch it, lest ye die. And the serpent said unto the woman, Ye shall not surely die: For God doth know that in the day ye eat thereof, then your eyes shall be opened and ye shall be as gods, knowing good and evil.

And when the woman saw that the tree was good for food, and that it was pleasant to the eyes, and a tree to be desired to make one wise, she took of the fruit thereof, and did eat, and gave also unto her husband with her, and he did eat.

(Genesis 3:1-6)

That single exposure to Satan was all that was needed to transmit the communicable disease of sin into the bloodline of all humanity. That initial contact quarantined mankind. It forced a wedge between the Creator and His creation.

SATAN'S STRATEGY

That fateful day in the Garden, Satan dangled before man the most basic of temptations: selfish desire. ''..*Ye shall be as Gods*..'' Although Adam had it all, the serpent easily enticed him with the notion of MORE.

Satan's attack was aimed at the two weakest parts of man's makeup: *the soul,* wherein resides the uniquely human attribute of free will, and *the flesh,* housing the sensory feelings that constantly influence the soul to do its physical bidding. These two elements are governed by man himself, thereby rendering them easily accessible to the serpent's vengeful ploy.

However, the third and most important ingredient of man, *the spirit,* was protected against Lucifer's game. This rare component of humanity was -- and remains -- the property of the Creator Himself. It is God's timeless means of communication with His creation.

The human spirit can be compared to a piano string which is perfectly tuned to a particular note. When another instrument sounds the exact same pitch, the tuned string will vibrate on its own. Likewise, when God sounds out His perfect will, man's eternal spirit acknowledges the communication. Humanity's created spirit *always* vibrates to the will of its Creator.

Nevertheless, this heavenly force does *not* override man's own free will. It allows humanity to make its own choices, right or wrong.

Although the spirit constantly, gently reverberates God's wishes, it *never* assumes control *until* man freely relinquishes that authority.

Realizing this, Satan quickly seized the physical side of Adam and put up a smoke screen of fleshly desire to distract his attention away from God's gentle call. To this day, Lucifer's diversions of pleasure (lust of the eye, lust of the flesh, pride of life) and pain (mental and physical disease) remain his only defense against man's free-will choice to follow God.

That extraordinary gift of free will not only separated Adam from earth's lower life forms, it now sadly severed his special bond of fellowship with God.

If that was not enough, his decision to disobey the Lord's one and only rule disqualified humanity's rights to God's perfect physical world, and by default, dominion fell into the corrupt hands of Lucifer.

In that regrettable instant, everything changed. The world that had once rumbled to life began to show signs of age. Everything about this physical sphere was suddenly in a state of decay.

...cursed is the ground for thy sake;
in sorrow shalt thou eat of it all the days

of thy life: Thorns also and thistles shall
it bring forth to thee; and thou shalt eat
the herb of the field; In the sweat of thy
face shalt thou eat bread, till thou return
unto the ground; for out of it wast thou
taken: for dust thou art, and unto dust
shalt thou return.

(Gen. 3: 17-19)

Flowers began to wither, rocks started to crumble and man's human body began to grow fragile with need, worry and pain. For Adam, Eve and the rest of mankind, the prognosis was all too obvious: Separation from God was indeed separation from life.

It seemed that Paradise was forever lost.

Nevertheless, though Satan's invasion gained him a piece of ground, the war that he started was far from over. Despite it all, the Creator (Who never changes) still desired a relationship with His creation. God's divine breath still resided within man's eternal spirit.

That day, the combat perimeters were drawn: God on one side, Satan on the other. And the scrimmage line dividing the two ran across the very heart of man; for within this one-of-a-kind creation resided the domains of *both* warring factions -- *spirit*, (the gift of God) and *flesh*, (the physical realm man relinquished to Satan).

Therefore, a divine strategy for humanity's rescue was conceived, and battle plans were drawn. On that decisive day, the voice of the Omniscient God spoke, and declared throughout the Garden the first of many prophecy/promises designed to give mankind hope and the serpent a reason to fear:

> *...I will put enmity between thee and the woman, and between thy seed and her seed: it shall bruise thy head and thou shalt bruise his heel.*
>
> *(Genesis 3:15)*

That day the war between spirit and flesh began.

"What began as a selfish act under
a tree... ended with a selfless act
on a tree."

GOD'S
RESCUE PLAN

"...Through the filter of the blood
covering, God, Our Physician, treated
the symptoms fo sin."

CHAPTER

II

Although God was displeased with the way man had used the gift of free will, He still loved His one-of-a-kind creation. The Lord knew that if things remained status-quo, man would be lost forever and would ultimately suffer the same fate that awaited Satan and his band of defectors. *Yet for divine fellowship to be restored, mankind had to be cleansed of the corruption it had contracted.*

Therefore, God devised a "two phased" purification process that would: (1.) initially allow Him closer contact to His tainted creation that He might tend to the physical symptoms of sin; (2.) introduce a cure which would totally annihilate sin itself and all of its diseased properties. And the one element common to both of these purification phases was *the shedding of blood.*

This liquid-like substance is the main ingredient of every living, breathing creation of God. Its vein-pulsing flow is the stuff which invigorates and sustains the very gift of physical existence. Its presence inside a body is the ultimate evidence of life.

However, if enough of the blood's potent ingredients are allowed to spill out of the body, the tangible presence of life itself also escapes. To put it in modern terms: blood, like gasoline, keeps the body's "motor" running. Without it, man's "earthsuit" is nothing but a lifeless shell.

Simply put, the substance of blood is the ultimate common denominator. Its presence, as well as its absence, affects the vital functions of both the *body* AND the *spirit.*

...for the life of all flesh is the blood...
(Leviticus 17:14)

Realizing the eternal value of this life-giving flow, God chose the element of blood as the "currency" (a promissory note of an agreed transaction) for His arrangements with man.

Phase One:
THE COVERING COVENANT

The first phase of the Creator's rescue plan was to narrow the breach that Satan had forged between God and man. Effecting this reconciliation would, by definition, require the two parties to come together. To achieve such a union, there had to be a measure of mutual agreement. Therefore, the Creator established a covenant with His creation and sealed it with the blood of a slaughtered animal.

It was necessary for man to agree with God and confess his disobedience. (Honesty makes mistakes easier to tolerate.) It was also important that humanity understood that "the wages of sin is death." (Romans 6:23) To accomplish this, God creatively employed a "visual aid" that graphically illustrated both the peril of sin and His divine promise to cover its corruption from His sight.

Upon tasting Eden's forbidden fruit, Adam and Eve immediately realized that they were naked. Their corruption to sin was exposed. Seeing their sad condition, God Himself slaughtered a beast and made coats of skin for the couple to wear. *The Lord shed the blood of an animal to provide a covering for humanity's transgression.*

> *Unto Adam also and to his wife did the Lord God make coats of skin, and clothed them.*
>
> *(Gen. 3:21)*

That event instituted the practice of animal sacrifice. Its purpose was to act as a *temporary blood covering* for man's transgressions. However, its effectiveness was so inadequate that our Old Testament forefathers had to repeat the process each time they brought a petition to The Lord. In effect, the shedding of animal blood was a means of "momentarily sterilizing'' man's sin infection, that he might re-establish limited contact with His Creator.

> *An altar of earth thou shalt make*
> *unto me, and thou shalt sacrifice thereon*
> *thy burnt offerings and thy peace offerings,*
> *thy sheep and thine oxen: in the places*
> *where I record my name I will come unto*
> *thee, and I will bless thee.*
>
> *(Exodus 20:24)*

God desired a one-on-one relationship with humanity. He longed to supply all of man's needs: spirit, soul and body. And through the covering of animal sacrifice, mankind was able to achieve a glimpse into the vast range of blessings the Father yearned to share.

In Exodus 15, the Israelites discovered that God was not only capable of rescuing them from the clutches of Pharaoh's army, He was also willing and able to supply their physical needs as well.

> *So Moses brought Israel from the*
> *Red Sea, and they went out into the*
> *wilderness of Shur; and they went three*
> *days in the wilderness and found no water.*
> *And when they came to Marah, they could*
> *not drink of the waters of Marah, for they*
> *were bitter...And the people murmured*
> *against Moses, saying, What shall we*
> *drink? And he (Moses) cried unto the*
> *Lord; and the Lord showed him a tree,*

which when he had cast into the waters,
the waters were made sweet.
                                    (Exodus 15:22-25)

Through that episode, Israel got a glimpse into the character of the Lord. On that day, they heard the voice of God, through Moses, declare; "...*I am the Lord that healeth thee.*" (Exodus 15:26) That powerful proclamation in the original Hebrew is translated "Jehovah-Rapha", which is to say - God Our Physician.

By such acts, it is obvious that the Lord wanted to be our helper and healer, but man's infection of sin impeded His efforts. Our exposure to Satan kept God at a distance. *The Lord's holy nature will not 'cohabitate' with corruption.* Therefore, the blood covering, the first step in the restoration process, became the temporary "filter" through which God worked.

Although He was unable to dwell eternally *within* the heart of man, the Lord still found a way to use the blood covering's limited access to His advantage. The Almighty God of the universe moved His living quarters "next door".

And let them make me a sanctuary;
that I may dwell among them.
                                    (Exodus 25:8)

From the Tabernacle's Holy of Holies, The Almighty was able to keep His distance yet still disperse His miracle working power. This was accomplished through His use of chosen, anointed (purified) individuals.

And Aaron (the High Priest) lifted up his hand toward the people, and blessed them, and came down from offering of the sin offering, and the burnt offering, and the peace offerings.... And there came a fire out from before the Lord, and consumed upon the altar the burnt offering and the fat: which when all the people saw, they shouted, and fell on their faces.
(Leviticus 9:22,24)

On another occasion when serpents entered Israel's camp and attacked the population, causing many to perish, God answered their cries for mercy through His servant Moses.

And the Lord said unto Moses, Make thee a fiery serpent, and set it upon a pole: and it shall come to pass, that every one that is bitten, when he looketh upon it, shall live. And Moses made a serpent of brass, and put it upon a pole, and it came to pass that if a serpent had bitten any man, when he beheld the serpent of brass, he lived.

(Numbers 21:8-9)

Throughout the Old Testament, God miraculously touched His people through the consecrated hands of His proxy representatives. The prophet Elijah, for instance, displayed his Master's desire to heal in a most dramatic way.

And it came to pass...that the son of the woman, the mistress of the house, fell sick; and his sickness was so sore, that there was no breath left in him. And she said unto Elijah, What have I to do with Thee, O thou man of God? Art thou come unto me to call my sin to remembrance, and to slay my son?

And he said unto her, Give me thy son. And he took him out of her bosom, and carried him up into a loft, where he abode, and laid him upon his own bed...And he stretched himself upon the child three times, and cried unto the Lord and said, O Lord my God, I pray thee, let this child's soul come into him again.

And the Lord heard the voice of Elijah, and the soul of the child came into him again, and he revived ...And the woman said to Elijah, Now by this I know that thou art a man of God, and that the word of the Lord in thy mouth is truth.

(1 Kings 17:17,18,19,21,24)

Just as God's healing power was displayed through Elijah, the authority of God was likewise demonstrated through His messenger Isaiah. This prophet's example was nothing short of earth-moving:

Standing over King Hezekiah's sickbed, Isaiah bluntly announced, *"Get your house in order, for thou shalt die, and not live."* Upon hearing these shocking words, the king turned his face to the wall and began to beseech God in tears.

Having delivered the Lord's message, the prophet was about to leave when suddenly God spoke to him and said:

> *"Turn again, and tell Hezekiah...I have heard thy prayer, and I have seen thy tears: behold, I will heal thee...and add unto thy days fifteen years..."*
>
> *(II Kings 20:5,6)*

Hearing Isaiah deliver this unexpected reprieve, the sick king became understandably doubtful. Realizing this, the prophet stated:

> *"This sign shalt thou have of the Lord, that the Lord will do the thing that he hath spoken: shall the shadow go forward ten degrees, or back ten degrees?"*

And Hezekiah answered,

> *"It is a light thing for the shadow to go down ten degrees: nay, but let the shadow return backward ten degrees."*
>
> *And Isaiah the prophet cried unto the Lord: and he brought the shadow ten degrees backward, by which it had gone down in the dial of Ahaz.*
>
> *(II Kings 20:9-11)*

Even through the "filter" of the blood covering and the use of His "go-betweens", the prophets, God was able to push back the shadow of sickness and death for all who recognized His authority. Nevertheless, this first phase of the Lord's purification process was nothing more than a "Band-aid". As a matter of fact, the New Testament book of Hebrews describes this first blood covenant as being, in a word, inadequate.

> *For if that first covenant had been faultless, then should no place have been sought for the second. For finding fault with them, he saith, Behold, the days come, saith the Lord, when I will make a new covenant with the house of Israel and with the house of Judah;*
>
> *(Hebrews 8:7-8)*

Man's free will decision changed God's paradise into Satan's partition. The corruption of sin which Adam allowed to infest the world restricted mankind's access to his Maker. Although The Lord longed for direct companionship with His creation, the first blood covenant could do very little to affect the barrier.

Through the filter of that covering, God, Our Physician, treated the symptoms of sin. But being merciful, He desired to do more than simply cover the corruption. God intended, from the foundation of the world, to cure the infestation!

From the beginning, His strategy was to break through Satan's barrier, eradicate sin and its puny arsenal of disease, and restore man to his rightful place of dominion.

However, this portion of God's rescue plan demanded a sacrificial covering far more potent than the blood of a soul-less animal. To eradicate the disease of sin, it would require a dose of *pure* blood from the same species that was originally infected -- man.

Phase Two:
THE SUBSTITUTE SACRIFICE

But man did not qualify. Humanity's bloodline was tainted from the very start by Adam's sin. The only alternative was to exchange man with a substitute that harbored the same rare combination of flesh and spirit. This replacement had to possess the qualities of a pure, sinless bloodline, and, as God so graphically illustrated with the first slaughtered animal, this alternative also had to shed its blood.

The sacrifice of this pure substitute would not have to be repeated. Its potent flow would supply, once and for all, the ultimate covering for all of humanity's transgressions.

Man's sin required a death. Man's sicknesses needed a cure. Yet, ironically, the only One Who could possibly fulfill all of these sanctified qualifications was the one, and the only -- Son of God!

Therefore, seeing that there was no other way to reconcile the earth and the creation He loved, The

Father Himself offered His Only Begotten to be the ultimate sacrifice.

Possessing the very Spirit of the Almighty, The Son honored the will of His Father. Clothing Himself in man's flesh through a virgin birth, Jesus Christ came to earth and became the soul supplier of what this temporal, imperfect world needed most: the healing balm of divine blood.

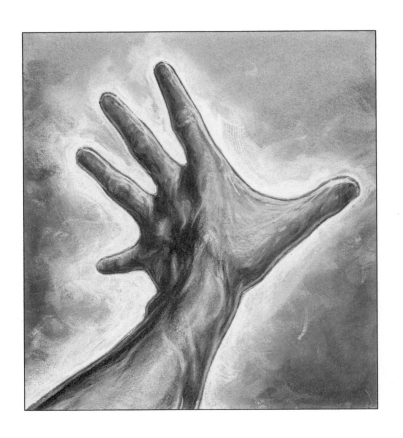

"Sin-infected humanity needed the kind of transfusion that only God could provide. And the only way such a divine exchange could be made was if God Himself provided the blood."

THE IMMUNIZED BLOOD OF JESUS

"That morning in Gethsemane's garden,
Christ, like the first Adam,
faced a hard choice."

CHAPTER

III

In today's modern society, the general public protects itself against the threat of disease by going to a family doctor for a vaccination. By exposing their bodies to the painful point of a syringe, they voluntarily allow their bloodstream to be injected with a portion of the *very illness* that they wish to avoid. The process is called immunization.

Modern medical science has learned that to fight a disease, it is sometimes necessary to be "infected" with it. And through this ironic process, the treated are rendered immune to the effects of a given illness.

Although this unusual method of prevention and healing is commonly used today, modern medicine is not the first to put its unique principles into practice. The process of *'deliberate infection to bring about immunity'* was described in graphic detail, over 2,700 years ago, by a man who never heard the word 'vaccination':

> *...He was wounded for our transgressions, he was bruised for our iniquities: the chastisement of our peace was upon him; and with his stripes we are healed...the Lord hath laid on Him the iniquity of us all.*
>
> *(Isaiah 53:5,6)*

Isaiah's emotional words painted a vivid portrait of an event that would ultimately take place some 700 years after his time. The old prophet looked into the future and described the torture and crucifixion of God's Own Son.

Not only do his words invoke an image of a painful death, they also provide a glimpse into the inner workings of The Creator's strategy. Although it was God's will to "immunize" the world against the contamination of Satan, The Lord knew that both His plan's success and Isaiah's prophecy would hinge on the outcome of yet *another* decision made in a garden, this time by a man called -- Jesus.

THE GARDEN BATTLEGROUND

Long before in Eden, Satan dangled before Adam the most basic of temptations, selfish desire. The blind, self-serving choice he made that day lured him into a grave. And eventually, all humanity stumbled in after him. Freely choosing to eat of the Tree of the Knowledge of Good and Evil, Adam got just what he asked for: the knowledge of every evil disease and atrocity, and the awareness of every good and perfect gift, which lay just beyond his infected reach.

But then Jesus entered the scene, armed with the mandate to "be about My Father's business".

One hundred percent man, one hundred percent God -- He came to earth with the power to heal and forgive. He spoke words of "Life" and light to those who had none. And He gave to all who would heed His words the will and the faith to climb out of their grave of despair.

However, when all was said and done, the paramount purpose of Jesus Christ was to be the substitutionary sacrifice for man's disobedience. It was His mission to administer the blood antidote for sin and disease to all of mankind.

Simply put, for God's plan to succeed, His only Son had to die.

In the early morning hours of that terrible-triumphant day, Jesus knowingly awaited His fate in the Garden of Gethsemane. Being the Son of God, He was aware of the torturous death He would soon face. Yet also being a man, and *in all points tempted like as we are..* (Heb.4:15), Jesus naturally wanted to avoid the whole painful situation.

Recalling Isaiah's graphic prophecy -- *"He was wounded for our transgressions...bruised for our iniquities: the chastisement of our peace was upon Him: and with His stripes we were healed... the Lord hath laid upon Him the iniquity of us all.."* --

(Isa. 54:5,6) the Son of God's physical mind contested the notion.

Within this "Second Adam", the domains of spirit and flesh also resided. There a battleground once again unfolded: God's plan on one side, Satan's selfish desire on the other.

That morning in Gethsemane's garden, Christ, like the first Adam, faced a *hard* choice. However, unlike the decision made in Eden, the alternatives that confronted Jesus would not only affect the world of the present and future, it would determine the ultimate fate of everyone, clear back to Adam himself.

> *And He went a little further, and fell on His face and prayed saying, O My Father, if it be possible, let this cup pass from me.*
>
> *(Mat.26:39)*

But instantaneously, His Spirit, in tune with The Father, voiced its rebuttal. And in almost the same breath, Christ immediately added: *"...Nevertheless, not as I will, but as thou wilt."*

There in that pivotal moment, (as He had throughout His earthly life), Jesus did not allow His temporal, physical body to make His decisions. He was indeed, "tempted as we are" -- *yet without sin.*

Instead of giving in to His physical, short-term desires, instead of surrendering to Satan's smoke screen of selfishness, Jesus listened to the Spirit of God within Him, and chose the path that would ultimately benefit both man and God for all eternity. Instantly, Christ gathered Himself and turned His attention back to the hour which He, Himself, said would come.

> *...For he shall be delivered unto the Gentiles, and shall be mocked and spitefully entreated, and spitted on; And they shall scourge him, and put him to death; and the third day he shall rise again.*
>
> *(Luke 18:32,33)*

CALVARY'S VACCINATION

Just as Christ prophesied, He was indeed delivered into the hands of the Gentiles. He was mocked and spat on. And after His robe was stripped from His shoulders, the snap of a Roman whip filled the morning air.

Just as the prophet Isaiah envisioned, The Son of God willingly endured the flesh tearing strokes of a leather cat o'nine tails. With each blood-letting incision, Jesus bore upon His back the nauseating agony of every disease mankind would ever know. He suffered through the intense torment of those thirty-nine lashes plus one, so we could boldly proclaim ...*with his stripes, we are healed*!

Led by His executioners up the steep incline of Calvary's hill, He was made to lie down on the long beam of the cross. There, He was forced to press the raw, open wounds of His back against the rough, splintery wood of a tree. His pain must have been excruciating.

However, on the backside of Calvary, between Christ and the cross, the miraculous was beginning. As His wounds began to flow against the skin of the tree, a crimson stain marked the post, thereby initiating God's definitive, redeeming *Passover of man's sicknesses and transgressions.*

Then, without warning, there came the sudden thud of a hammer.

The nails that pounded into Christ's hands and feet that day "injected" Him with every blatant iniquity, every subtle sin, every vile act that mankind had ever or would ever commit.

...the Lord hath laid upon him the iniquity of us all...

Hanging from those nails, Jesus was also deliberately infected with all manner of sickness and sin, so to bring about salvation and healing, through His divine, immunized blood.

For this purpose, Jesus came into the world. Humanity needed the kind of transfusion that only God could provide. And the only way such a divine exchange could be made was if God Himself provided the blood.

The Son of God became our substitute. He suffered the penalty of our sins and died in our place. He endured the ill effects of Calvary's "vaccination" so that we wouldn't have to. And by simply believing in

Him and the power of His blood, we can be cleansed from our unrighteousness AND *healed of all manner of sickness and disease.*

The Apostle Peter put it this way:

> *...Christ also suffered for us... who his own self bare our sins in his own body on the tree, that we, being dead to sins, should live unto righteousness: by whose stripes ye were healed...*
>
> *(1 Peter 2:21,24)*

Notice that Peter said that we *"were"* healed. And Isaiah said that you *"are"* healed. Therefore, if you *were* and you **are,** that means that your body *IS ALREADY healed,* present tense!

If you will only believe in the power of His blood and accept what Christ has done for you on the cross, *YOU CAN BE HEALED* right now, present tense! *TODAY!*

THE BACK SIDE OF CALVARY

Before Calvary, man had to approach the Lord through the "filter" of animal blood and the veil of God's "go-betweens", the Temple High Priest and prophets. There was no direct contact. And Although God wanted, and man needed, this separation to end, the original blood covenant could not fulfill that purpose.

However on the backside of Calvary, when the blood of Christ's sacrifice stained the rough skin of that tree, all the sin and sickness which Adam brought into the world, upon touching God's forbidden tree, was - COVERED. With His sacrifice, there is no more need for the old covenant; Christ's selfless act took care of it all.

Neither by the blood of goats and calves, but by His own blood he entered in once into the holy place having obtained eternal redemption for us.

(Hebrews 9:12)

The sin-infection Adam contracted by his selfish act under a tree was covered for all time by Christ's selfless act on a tree.

Through the ultimate sacrifice of Christ, all the barriers came tumbling down. With His triumphant cry, "It is finished!", the breach which Satan had thrust between man and God was destroyed, and the temple veil of the Holy of Holies was ripped in two.

Jesus, when he had cried again with a loud voice, yielded up the ghost. And behold, the veil of the temple was rent in twain from the top to the bottom; and the earth did quake and the rocks rent;

(Matthew 27: 50,51)

Satan was once again booted out, and no barrier of separation, save man's own free will, now stood between The Creator and His creation.

> *There is therefore now no condemnation to them which are in Christ Jesus, who walk not after the flesh, but after the Spirit...For what the law could not do, in that it was weak through the flesh, God sending His Own Son in the likeness of sinful flesh, and for sin, condemned sin in the flesh.*
>
> *(Romans 8:1,3)*

Now, safe on the back side of Calvary, our sin and sicknesses are covered once and for all; for Christ took all of our corruption with Him to the grave. And when He rose to life again, our Savior left our sins buried there, covered for time and eternity!

On the back side of Calvary, there's no reason to endure the condemnation of your past or suffer the discomfort of your physical maladies. By simply believing in the redeeming "transfusion" power of Christ's blood, you can bury it all and be resurrected again, to a *renewed* life: body, soul and spirit.

The Apostle Paul put it this way:

> *Therefore if any man be in Christ, he is a new creature: old things are passed away; behold, all things are become new.*
>
> *(2 Corinthians 5:17)*

Jesus Christ accomplished everything that God the Father started at the creation, and that includes total health, and a fulfilled one-on-one relationship with the Creator Himself. And all that you need to do to acquire these gifts is excerise your free will.

If healing was available to those separated by the old covenant, just think how much more accessible it is now that we're on the back side of Calvary. Now, all that is needed to apply this heavenly balm is pure and simple faith.

When you go to your family doctor and expose your body to the prick of a vaccination needle, you are blindly trusting that the disease he is injecting into your bloodstream will keep you from illness...*that's faith*!

With just a portion of that "believing power", (even as small as a mustard seed), you not only can have the assurance of health, but you can also have the promise of eternal life.

If Adam can change the entire world with a decision, and Christ, by choosing the way of the Spirit, could repair the damage, just think how your world could change if you would only choose.

All you have to do is simply believe that:

...he was wounded for our transgressions, he was bruised for our iniquities: the chastisement of our peace was upon him; and with his stripes we are healed.

(Isaiah 53:5)

"As the wounds on His back pressed
against the rough wood of the tree,
a crimson stain marked the post,
thereby initiating God's Passover
of man's sicknesses and
transgressions."

SIMPLY BELIEVE

"...God did not lay down His Son's life so that
our beat up 'earthsuits' could sit in
Heaven's front yard and rust."

CHAPTER
I V

Although most Christians understand what took place in the garden of Eden, and though the majority comprehend God's sacrificial plan to save mankind, there are still those today who fail to grasp that healing was -- *and is* -- a part of God's divine design.

Salvation and healing are two gifts wrapped up in the same package. For God, it is just as easy to forgive sin as it is to dissolve a cancerous growth. To Him, *healing* is just as important and necessary as Salvation.

The apostle Mark brought this point into vivid focus in his re-telling of the day Jesus healed the man with the palsy:

And they come unto him (Jesus), bringing one sick of the palsy, which was borne of four. And when they could not come nigh unto him for the press, they

*uncovered the roof where he was: and
when they had broken it up, they let down
the bed wherein the sick of the palsy lay.
When Jesus saw their faith, he said unto
the sick of the palsy, Son, thy sins be
forgiven thee.   But there were certain of
the scribes sitting there, and reasoning in
their hearts, Why doth this man thus speak
blasphemies?   Who can forgive sins but
God only?*

*...when Jesus perceived in his spirit
that they so reasoned within themselves,
he said unto them, Why reason ye these
things in your heart?   Whether is it easier
to say to the sick of the palsy, Thy sins be
forgiven thee; or to say, Arise, take up
thy bed, and walk?   But that ye may know
that the Son of Man hath power on earth
to forgive sins, (he saith to the sick of the
palsy), I say unto thee, Arise, and take up
thy bed, and go thy way into thine house.*

*And immediately he arose, took up
the bed, and went forth before them all;
insomuch that they were all amazed, and
glorified God, saying, We never saw it on
this fashion.*

(Mark 2:3-12)

Thanks to the displayed power of God's Son, the
man who came in with his back on his bed left with

his bed on his back! And the only thing the scribes could do was grumble.

Like oil and water, Jesus and religion have never mixed well. Back in the New Testament days, when Christ held out a healing hand, the scribes and Pharisees squirmed uncomfortably. Although they didn't like what He was doing, they could not publicly challenge His work, for the evidence of opened eyes and straightened limbs were widespread and irrefutable.

However, when Jesus spoke of forgiving sin, the religious community presumed that it finally had Him cornered. But as always, Christ was one step ahead of the devil's game.

To display the full range of His authority, The Son of God pointed a loaded question at His adversaries: "Is it easier to say 'your sins are forgiven', or 'take up your bed and walk?'"

Knowing that religion always needs tangible proof, Jesus did not wait for an answer. Immediately, He turned to the palsied man and spoke, *"Arise and take up thy bed."*

Christ's words spoke power and life to the palsied man's limbs. And when he stood to his feet, religion had its tangible proof that not only could Jesus heal, but by extension, His Words possessed the power to forgive as well.

Although twenty centuries have passed, Jesus and religion still do not mix. Christ hasn't changed; man has. In the New Testament days, the theological world conceded that the power of healing existed and balked at the forgiveness of sin. But today, it's the other way around. The church doesn't seem to mind preachers talking about Salvation and forgiveness of sin, but they are adamant against any positive reference to the subject of divine healing.

It's a sad commentary on today's bible believers, but a large portion of them do not receive the healing they need, simply because they are too busy wondering, *"Is it God's will to heal?"*

That question was only voiced once in the New Testament. The inquiry was posed by a humble leper, kneeling at the feet of God's Son, during the first year of His ministry.

"If Thou wilt," the man submissively bowed, "Thou canst make me clean."

Looking down at the man's white, flaky skin, Jesus was moved with compassion. And stretching out His hand, Christ gently touched the leper and answered, *"I will, be thou clean."*

Instantly, as the man rose to his feet, the surface of his tainted skin became as soft and pure as a baby's. And excitedly,

> *...he went out, and began to publish it much, and to blaze abroad the matter, insomuch that Jesus could no more openly enter into the city, but was without in desert places: and they came to Him from every quarter.*
>
> *(Mark 1:45)*

After that day, the overwhelming crowds that surrounded Jesus made it obvious why the question of healing was only asked once. The news of His compassion and power was indeed "blazed abroad".

However, these days, it seems there are still churches that haven't grasped the Good News. These worthless institutions are so busy expounding their own agenda that they fail to even bring up the subject of healing, much less practice it.

If that's not bad enough, there are sermons being preached from today's pulpits that proclaim the validity of salvation by the Blood, yet simultaneously reduce the experience of healing to mere coincidence.

Looking at the results of such unproductive congregations, it's no wonder that there are still those who ask, "Is God even *able* to heal?"

Able?! He flung the stars into place and traced out the course of rivers with His finger. He set the world spinning upside down and commanded the oceans not to spill a drop.

Is He able? He walked on the water. He turned water into wine and commanded the wind and the waves to be still. He fed five thousand with a few loaves and fishes and drove out devils with a single word.

Is Jesus able? Ask blind Bartimaeus to describe the Savior's smile. Ask the widow if her tainted blood is still an issue. Ask Lazarus what it's like to be called back from the other side.

He took up another man's cross and placed on His shoulders the weight of the entire world's sin and disease. He willingly allowed His immunized blood to be spilled for our salvation and healing. And He rose again that we, too, might be transformed by His power and grace.

Is Jesus able? A man once brought his demon tortured son to the disciples for healing. But despite their collective, diligent efforts, Christ's apostles were powerless to control the convulsing lad. Finally, just as the boy's disappointed father was about to turn for home, Jesus, (Who is always right on time), came on the scene.

Assessing the situation, The Son of God instantly took control: *"Bring him to me..."*

That's good advice! When the doctors can't help you; when your lawyer's hands are tied; when the deacons shrug their shoulders; and the bank president shakes his head "no", bring your problems to Jesus. He is more than willing; He is able to repair the damage.

It amazes me. In the midst of a crisis, people compulsively grab at every fad, fable and "snake-oil remedy" within reach and totally ignore the spiritual power that is at their disposal. Such disabled people remind me of an old nursery rhyme:

Humpty-Dumpty sat on a wall.
Humpty-Dumpty had a great fall.
All the King's horses,

And all the King's men
Couldn't put Humpty together again.

Why was the repair job given to the King's horses and men? Why wasn't the matter brought directly to the King? He's the one with the power.

Likewise, Jesus is "the way" to The Father, the Creator of all things. When your body isn't functioning correctly, who better is there to turn to than the One Who created you?

The watch on my arm is proof positive that somewhere there is a watchmaker. If my timepiece suddenly stops or requires replacement parts, the best thing for me to do is to find the man who made the watch. He is the one best able to fix the damage. Just the same - the healing power of Christ's immunized blood was designed specifically to repair whatever malady that keeps you from ticking.

No matter how desperate your situation seems to be, don't grab for fads, fables or a quick fix; like the man with the demon possessed son, bring your problems to Jesus.

> *And they brought him unto him: and*
> *when he (the Jesus) saw him (the boy),*
> *straightway the spirit tare him; and he*
> *fell on the ground, and wallowed foaming.*
> *And He (Jesus) asked his father, How long*
> *is it ago since this came unto him? And*
> *he said, Of a child. And ofttimes it hath*
> *cast him into the fire and into the waters*
> *to destroy him: but if thou canst do*

anything, have compassion on us, and help us.

Jesus said unto him, If thou canst believe, all things are possible to him that believeth.

And straightway the father of the child cried out, and said with tears, Lord, I believe; help thou mine unbelief.

When Jesus saw that the people came running together, he rebuked the foul spirit, saying unto him, Thou dumb and deaf spirit, I charge thee, come out of him, and enter no more into him. And the spirit cried, and rent him (the boy) sore, and came out of him: and he was as one dead; insomuch that many said, He is dead. But Jesus took him by the hand, and lifted him up; and he arose.

(Mark 9:20-27)

That day, Jesus displayed to the people that *He* was not only available and willing to heal, but that He was also indeed "*able*". Furthermore, if you look at this episode closely, you'll also discover that Christ clearly gave us a glimpse of *our own capabilities*, as well. He said,

...If thou canst believe, all things are possible...

If you can *simply believe* in the power of God, there is nothing -- absolutely *no* thing -- that you cannot do. There is no problem you cannot influence. There is no circumstance you cannot change.

If God can speak and create an entire world out of the vacuum of space, there is no reason to doubt that He can call into existence whatever you need.

The only limitations God has are the ones that you place on Him. If you question His willingness; if you doubt His ability, or even your own worthiness; you are constricting the flow of His miracle-working power.

His willingness was illustrated when He voluntarily hung on the cross. Your worthiness was exhibited plainly by the blood He shed there. And Jesus Christ's unlimited ability was demonstrated profoundly when He emerged from a tomb of death triumphant, alive forever more!

When Mom and Dad can't seem to find the answer; when husbands and wives can offer no hope or comfort; when it seems that your Humpty-Dumpty world has shattered into thousands of irreplaceable pieces; when everything that can be done *has* been done - have faith and bring your problems to the Master Watchmaker, The King of kings.

When you get right down to the heart of the matter, *it's not a question of what He can do, but rather a question of what YOU can believe.* The Old Testament story of the Shunammite woman is a perfect example of this kind of faith.

This elderly woman wanted to be so close -- so dependent -- on God that she asked her husband to

build a room onto their house for the traveling prophet,
Elisha.

> *"... I know this is a man of God,*
> *who passes by us regularly. Please, let*
> *us make a small upper room on the wall:*
> *and let us put a bed for him there, and a*
> *table and a chair and a lampstand: so it*
> *will be, whenever he comes to us, he can*
> *turn in there."*
>
> *(II Kings 4: 9-10 NKJ)*

The Shunammite's idea seemed good to her husband. They had often heard Elisha speak during his
regular visits to town.   In fact, gradually, over the
years, it had become a steady practice for the prophet
to go home with the couple for dinner and fellowship.

Elisha was *his* generation's link to God. Naturally, with that kind of divine connection, the old couple
wanted him near. So they knocked down a wall, hung
a door and constructed an adjoining room to their house
for the prophet.

Doing so, this family in Shunem (which means
"double resting place") *joined their house to the house
of God.* By attaching their home to God's, they not
only had a place to rest, they could also "rest assured"
(have faith) that no matter what may come, the Lord
God Almighty was *able* and *available* to help them,
because -- He was right next door!

When the Shunammites presented Elisha with
his comfortable quarters, the prophet was moved. Lying

on his new bed, he pondered what could be done to show his appreciation. Nevertheless, after much thought and consideration, no solution seemed adequate. Eventually running out of ideas, the prophet then turned to his servant, Gehazi:

> ...And he said, "What then is to be done for her?" And Gehazi answered, "Verily, she has no child, and her husband is old."
>
> (II Kings 4:14)

The house was indeed empty. There were no children. Noting his servant's keen observation, Elisha immediately called for the old woman.

> ...And when he had called her, she stood in the door. And he said, "About this season, according to the time of life, thou shalt embrace a son." And she said, "Nay, my lord, thou man of God, do not lie to thine handmaid."
>
> (II Kings 4:15,16)

Her initial reaction should not be interpreted as doubt, but more appropriately, as total surprise. The woman's words were a genuine response to a statement that definitely seemed "un"-natural. She was indeed far past the *natural* time for motherhood. And likewise, there was no denying that her husband was an old man.

Nevertheless, when God decides to do something, the standard rules of creation are suspended. When He says a certain thing will occur, nature voluntarily relinquishes its jurisdiction and bows its authority to the Creator's wishes, thereby making mere nature -- Super-natural!

Mankind could take some pointers from nature: If we would simply believe and likewise relinquish ourselves to God's wishes, the supernatural could be *our* everyday nature too. Remember, *it's not a question of what God can do; it's a question of what you can believe.*

> *And the woman conceived, and bare a son at that season that Elisha had said to her, according to the time of life. And when the child was grown, it fell on a day, that he went out to his father to the reapers. And he said to his father, "My head, my head". And he (the father) said to a lad, "Carry him to his mother." And when he had taken him, and brought him to his mother, he (the boy) sat on her knees till noon, and then died.*
>
> *(II Kings 4:17-20)*

In that devastating instant, the Shunammite woman had every reason to cry out and question God; her miracle son was dead. However, instead of erupting into an understandable display of motherly remorse, she chose to handle her problem a different way;

> *And she went up, and laid him on the bed of the man of God, and shut the door upon him, and went out.*
>
> *(II Kings 4:21)*

66

This stalwart woman took her problem to the
Lord and left it there.

*And she called unto her husband,
and said, "Send me, I pray thee, one of
the young men, and one of the asses, that
I may run to the man of God, and come
again." And he said, "Wherefore wilt
thou go to him today? It is neither new
moon, nor sabbath." And she said, "It
shall be well."*

(II Kings 4:22-23)

The old woman had such faith, that she didn't
even bother to tell her husband the devastating news.
She had places to go, appointments to keep. She had
to see a certain Watchmaker about repairing one of
His custom creations.

Unlike the man who brought his devil-tormented
son to the disciples, the Shunammite did not waste
time or energy with those who could do *nothing* about
her problem. No snake-oil cures for her; she was
taking the broken pieces of her dilemma straight to
The King Himself.

I like what she told her husband; ''It shall be
well." *Its not a question of what God can do, it's a
question of what You can believe.*

Then she saddled an ass, and said to her servant,
''Drive, and go forward; slack not thy riding for me;
except I bid thee." So she went and came unto the
man of God to Mount Carmel.

*And it came to pass, when the man
of God saw her afar off, that he said to
Gehazi his servant, "Behold, yonder is
that Shunammite: Run now, I pray thee,
to meet her, and say unto her, Is it well
with thee?   Is it well with thy husband?
Is it well with the child?"...*

(II Kings 4:24-26)

Any other time, Gehazi's question would have
been considered polite banter between old friends, but
on this occasion, his inquiry had the same volatile
potential as a keg of dynamite - with a short fuse. But
again, the woman's strong, stubborn faith sustained
her. ...And she answered, *"It is well."*(II Kings 4:26)

*And when she came to the man of
God to the hill, she caught him by the
feet: but Gehazi came near to thrust her
away.   And the man of God said, "Let
her alone; for her soul is vexed within
her: and the Lord hath hid it from me,
and hath not told me."*

*Then she said, "Did I desire a son of
my lord?   did I not say, Do not deceive
me?"*

*Then he (Elisha) said to Gehazi,
"Gird up thy loins, and take my staff in
thine hand, and go thy way: If thou meet
any man, salute him not; and if any salute
thee, answer him not again: and lay my
staff on the face of the child."*

*And the mother of the child said,
"As the Lord liveth, and thy soul liveth,
I will not leave thee." And he arose, and
followed her.*

(II Kings 4:27-30)

Having joined her house to the house of God, the
Shunammite knew what God could do. After all, *He*
was the One Who gave her the miracle child. Therefore, she was not about to entrust her son to Gehazi,
Elisha's staff, or to any of the King's horses or men.
She stubbornly clung to the feet of God's earthly rep-
resentative and demanded nothing short of a command
performance. Her faith compelled Elisha to follow.

*And Gehazi passed on before them,
and laid the staff upon the face of the
child; but there was neither voice, nor
hearing. Wherefore he (Gehazi) went
again to meet him (Elisha), and told him,
saying, "The child is not awakened." And
when Elisha was come into the house,
behold, the child was dead, and laid upon
his bed.*

*He went in, therefore, and shut the
door upon them twain, and prayed unto
the Lord. And he went up, and lay upon
the child, and put his mouth upon his
mouth, and his eyes upon his eyes, and
his hands upon his hands; and he stretched*

*himself upon the child: and the flesh of
the child waxed warm....*

(II Kings 4:31-34)

When your faith allows God to get involved in
your situation, His healing flow always has a way of
warming things up.

*Then he (Elisha) returned, and
walked in the house to and fro; and went
up, and stretched himself upon him (the
boy): and the child sneezed... and the
child opened his eyes.*

*And he called Gehazi, and said,
"Call the Shunammite." So he called her.
And when she was come unto him, he
said, "Take up thy son." Then she went
in, and fell at his feet, and bowed herself
to the ground, and took up her son, and
went out."*

(II Kings 4:35-37)

I admire that old woman for not only did she
display a monumental faith, she also exhibited a great
capacity for praise. If this tragedy had happened to
one of *my* children, Ashton or Austin, and the prophet
announced, "Here's your child", I would have immediately rushed to the bed and wrapped my arms around
them - *first*. But that's not what the Shunammite did.
She fell down at Elisha's feet, bowed herself to the
ground and gave thanks to God for giving her miracle
child life once again. *Then* she picked up her boy.

Furthermore, throughout her ordeal, the old woman proclaimed, *"It shall be well."* That powerful statement did not question the situation; it did not evaluate God's ability or His willingness to intervene. It simply proved that the old Shunammite woman indeed lived in a "double resting place". She was able to "rest assured" that God was just as available to her as if He lived next door, and that her miracle was not predicated by what He could do, but rather on what she was willing to believe.

The old woman simply displayed her faith and left the hard part up to God.

THE HARD PART

It has been said that religion is the practice of making simple things hard. Never has that theology been more in vogue than it is today. It seems that our modern world finds it increasingly difficult to comprehend that God will supply our every need -- if we but simply ask and believe.

The fact is that Satan (still trying to get back at God) has slyly placed the notion in the collective rationale of modern man that to receive anything from God we must go through the torturous mechanics of meaningless rituals. That old serpent had perpetuated the idea that to gain God's ear one must articulate certain words, dance a pre-choreographed jig, and fulfill a specific set of rules. But my friends, that evil notion is the farthest thing from the truth!

There is no need to go through the rituals and formulas of man or the sacrifices of religion. It isn't difficult to get to God. In fact, He's already taken care of the hard part for you.

Through the death of Jesus Christ, we can be reconciled to God and actually have an intimate, personal relationship with the Creator. The only requirement is *faith* in the fact that Christ accomplished this for *you*.

Through the blood Jesus sacrificed on Calvary's tree, you can be cleansed of every physical sickness, discomfort and disease; every form of mental anguish and torture; and all manner of infirmity. The only prerequisite is to *believe*.

It is that simple. The hard part has already been tackled. *If God didn't want to heal you, He should not have done it*! Remember, *by his stripes, you WERE healed*! Your cure has already been appropriated, through the immunized blood of His Son.

Whether you accept God's gift or not is up to you. All it takes is faith - which is the *absolute absence* of doubt.

When you question the notion of healing, you're not wondering if God will heal you, you're wondering if He's lying. That's unbelief. The Bible says that "*I am the God that healeth thee*." That's not a denomination's word; it's God's Word.

Why would He put into motion a battle plan to redeem you from sin and not make provisions to cleanse you of sin's disrepair? Why would God sacrifice His Only Son to rectify His relationship with a sickly, diseased creation?

A man does not lay down good money for a rusty, beat-up jalopy unless he knows he can tune it up, shine it up and get it back on the road. Likewise, God did not lay down His Son's life so that our beat-up "earthsuits" could sit in Heaven's front yard and rust.

If you are saved by the blood of Jesus Christ and you know it, you're redeemed! You are on your way to Heaven. Sin's curse is broken. Therefore, if you believe God's Word on Salvation, there's no reason why you should not believe that you are also healed.

The same immunized blood that saved your soul was shed as well for the healing of your body. This is not just a factual promise; it's a Bible truth.

What is the difference between fact and truth? *Facts are temporal*; they can falter. The scientific community is always updating their information. More often than not, when their influx of data is amended and the details of their studies are analyzed, the house of cards they've built with facts usually falls.

On the other hand, *truth is eternal*, an absolute. It is a reality of fixed law which has been established from the beginning of time itself.

Forever, O Lord, Psalms 119:89 proclaims, *thy word is settled in heaven.*

God's word never changes. He is the Way, the *Truth* and the Life. Every syllable of prophecy in the scriptures has been fulfilled. Everything that God said would happen up to this day *has* happened without fail.

His Words are Life. When He speaks, it is always the truth - and the truth cannot be changed.

If your doctor tells you that you have only six weeks to live, don't worry; he's just reporting the temporal facts. Instead of panicking, you should start praising, for temporal facts can never stand up to God's eternal Word.

> *I create the fruit of the lips; Peace,*
> *peace to him that is far off, and to him*
> *that is near, saith the Lord; and I will*
> *heal him.*
>
> *(Isaiah 57:19)*

In the midst of adversity, you *can* have peace. No matter where you are, near or far, in a church pew or lying on a surgeon's table, God's words of truth and healing are potent and available.

> *He sent His word, and healed them,*
> *and delivered them from their destructions.*
>
> *(Psalms 107:20)*

If you will simply listen to God's truth rather than to man's facts, you can easily tap into His heavenly healing benefits.

This gift from God requires only our simple participation to gain its benefits. Though you are not responsible to perform your healing, it is a basic re-

74

quirement, however, that you initiate your miracle by *displaying* your belief. Faith will not work without corresponding actions.

ACTION = EXPECTATION

Throughout both the Old and New Testaments, God demanded that the sick *act* on their belief in His healing power, so that His supernatural flow might be released. A good example of this process is found in the story of Naaman.

As the victorious Captain of Syria's armies, Naaman was a tough man and held great favor with his king. However, Naaman was also a leper. Upon hearing of Israel's God, he was sent by his king to visit the nation and inquire if anything could be done to relieve his malady. Hearing about Naaman's plight, the prophet Elisha sent a message to the Syrian Captain. The prophet simply told Naaman to...

Go and wash in the Jordan (river)
seven times, and thy flesh shall come again
to thee, and thou shalt be clean.
(II Kings 5:10)

Just like many in today's society, Naaman was somewhat put out by Elisha's uncomplicated request. To this Syrian Captain, the prophet's informality was confusing.

*...I thought, He will surely come out
to me, and stand, and call on the name of
the Lord his God, and strike his hand
over the place, and recover the leper. Are
not Abana and Pharpar, rivers of
Damascus, better than all the waters of
Israel? May I not wash in them, and be
clean? So he turned and went away in a
rage.*

(II Kings 5:11-12)

The muddy state of the Jordan River had nothing to do with Naaman's healing. The real issue here was his stubborn state of mind. It took one of his own servants to finally show him that he was making something easy into something hard.

*...if the prophet had bid thee do some
great thing, wouldest thou not have done
it? How much rather then, when he saith
to thee, Wash, and be clean?*

(II Kings 5:13)

Seeing his servant's logic, Naaman calmed down and turned toward the river.

*Then went he down, and dipped
himself seven times in the Jordan,
according to the saying of the man of
God: and his flesh came again like unto
the flesh of a child, and he was clean.*

(II Kings 5:14)

Coming up out of the muddy water that first time, nothing changed. Likewise, breaking the surface a second time didn't seem to make any difference. Three, four, five, even six times more Naaman immersed himself in the Jordan, but nothing happened. However, when he broke the water line the seventh and final time, something miraculous took place; he was clean! The Syrian Captain's healing came only *after* he obeyed.

To obey someone, you have to believe in him. Therefore, *the act of obedience is a form of faith.* And faith is God's only requirement for healing.

When we act on our faith, we display our *expectation* that healing is on the way.

Christ's healing of the man's withered hand, in Matthew 12:13, was manifested only after the man took an *active* role - and did some stretching.

Remember, the atmosphere of expectation is the birthplace of miracles. And never was that atmosphere more highly charged than the day Jesus passed by an ailing woman who suffered with an issue of blood.

Like the man with the deformed hand, this woman's protracted predicament had long since withered away all hope for her recovery. The woman's situation seemed terminal, irreversible - up until that day Jesus passed by.

And a woman having an issue of blood twelve years, which had spent all of her living upon physicians, neither could be healed of any, came behind Him and touched the border of His garment:

77

and immediately her issue of blood stanched.

And Jesus said, Who touched me?...I perceive that virtue is gone out of me...and falling down before Him, she declared unto Him before all the people for what cause she had touched Him, and how she was healed immediately. And He said unto her, Daughter, be of good comfort: thy faith hath made thee whole; go in peace.

(Luke 8:43-48)

Using what little energy she had, this woman fought a large crowd just to touch the clothes of Jesus. What made this frail woman do such a thing? *Expectation.*

Watching Christ and His large group of followers pass by, the ailing woman began to think on all that she had heard about this Man of Miracles. She recalled how He had opened blind eyes and caused the lame to walk. As she thought on these things, the notion began to well up in her spirit that if He could do those things for others, Jesus could change her circumstances, too.

Sparked by that *belief,* she sprang to her feet, and *acted* on it. Stepping into the passing crowd, the woman began to push and shove her way through the pack. With each step, her faith increased. Ignoring twelve painful years of disappointment, she fixed her eyes on the Man up front, and elbowed her way forward.

Finally, the sick woman came within reach of God's Son. Extending her arm toward Him through the bump and jostle of the crowd, the woman with the issue of blood strained and stretched until her spindly fingers caught hold of Christ's garment.

Upon contact, her twelve-year-old disorder immediately disappeared. *In that instant, the disease which had tainted her blood was no longer an issue.*

You don't reach out for something unless you *expect* to get it.

This determined woman stretched out her hand, and by that *act,* she communicated to her situation her strong belief in the power of Jesus Christ. By that demonstration of faith, her irreversible circumstances *changed.*

"One hand reached for a tree...
another was nailed to it."

SPEAK THE WORD

"If the Lord and His Word never change,
and if He created life with a spoken
thought, then He is still able
to speak into existence
whatever you need today."

CHAPTER

V

Satan never relinquishes his stronghold over you just because you are uncomfortable. You have to show him who's boss. And nothing gets your message across faster than when you reach out, speak the name of Jesus and *expect* an answer.

In the middle of a tempestuous, wave-crashing storm, the apostle Peter called on Christ's name. However, the extraordinary thing about *this* particular petition is that he *actually believed* that Jesus would answer it!

...The boat was already a considerable distance from land, buffeted by the waves because the wind was against it. During the fourth watch of the night Jesus went out to them, walking on the lake. When the disciples saw him walking on the lake they were terrified. "It's a

ghost" they said, and cried out in fear.
But Jesus immediately said to them: Take
courage! It is I. Don't be afraid."
  "Lord if it is you," Peter replied,
tell me to come to you on the water."
  "Come," He said. Then Peter got
down out of the boat, walked on the water
and came toward Jesus.
         (Matthew 14:24-31 TLB)

Hearing the answer to his incredible request, Peter threw his leg over the side of the wind-tossed ship and lowered himself *onto* the sea. His actions were simple, yet powerful.

Having faith in Jesus, Simon Peter ignored the roaring waves and literally acted as if it were a common, everyday occurrence to do the impossible.

He didn't dance any jig or offer up an animal sacrifice; Peter simply threw his leg over the side -- as if he were *actually* going somewhere!

His faith, coupled with The Son of God's one word, "Come", pushed all indecision out of the picture. And instantly, all of the necessary elements locked into place to allow a mere human being to walk on water.

The power of faith is simply concentrating more on what *you and God can do* to the waves, than what the waves can do to you.

Take, for example, Craig and Judy Bickle. For this young couple, it seemed the waves were far too high. The storm they faced almost pulled them under.

As a matter of fact, the doctor's report claimed that Craig was, ''...drowning from the inside out.''

BELIEVING IS CONCEIVING

A stabbing pain in his lungs yanked him from his sleep. In an instant, Craig was sitting straight up in bed.

Awakened by the commotion, Judy opened her eyes and slowly became aware of her husband's strange gasping. In their two years of marriage, he had never shown any sign of illness. In fact, Craig had never been sick a day in all of his 25 years, that is, until *that* moment.

At the Emergency Room, a chaotic parade of doctors, nurses, tubes and needles surrounded the young man. In the waiting room, Judy was likewise encompassed by her concerned family. In the wee hours of that morning, they held each other and hoped.

Evaluating their results, the medical staff considered a number of possibilities, but eventually the prognosis was clear -- young Craig Bickle had fallen victim to acute pneumonia.

Under normal conditions, such news would have been tragic, but for this twosome, the diagnosis was especially crushing; for close to three months, the Bickles had been attending our church, World Harvest, where divine healing is proclaimed in every service.

In fact, only two weeks before the appearance of Craig's illness, the couple publicly experienced the baptism of the Holy Spirit in the church's sanctuary. Therefore, when the doctor calmly stated: *"...you're drowning from the inside out; you are not going to make it."*, the Bickle's natural reaction was despair, questions and doubt.

"Here we are Lord", Judy whispered, "we've given our lives to you; we've been filled with Your Spirit; - and now *this* happens to my husband?"

When they exchanged their dry, denominational background for the faith-filled atmosphere of World Harvest Church, the Bickles felt they had been given a new lease on life. There they had witnessed first-hand unexplainable miracles. And they had taken to heart the Spirit-led messages that were preached every time the doors were opened.

But now in the hospital, it seemed that the doctor's devastating words echoed louder than God's word. It looked as though the small print in their new lease-on-life concealed a clause of "early eviction".

Medically, the only recourse was to drain the pneumatic fluid from Craig's infected lungs. This continual process kept him alive, but it also weakened his respiratory system. In no time, Judy's once robust husband was seventy pounds thinner.

Although I frequently visited his hospital bed-side with words of expectation and encouragement, the tangible evidence of Craig's dwindling condition could not - *and would not* - be ignored.

With each labored breath, the ailing young Christian and his wife found it harder to conceive the notion of Simon Peter's kind of faith. It was a struggle.

Alone one Wednesday evening, Judy entered the sanctuary of the Church. Late for the service, she slipped into a space on the back pew and listened to the upbeat choruses resounding over the clapping, hand-waving crowd. Having spent so many hours in the antiseptic solitude of a hospital, she felt good to be in such an energetic, positive atmosphere.

Suddenly the music stopped. As the reverberations faded, the young housewife recognized a familiar voice coming thorough the sanctuary speakers. And after a moment, she realized that the voice was speaking to - her!

"Judy!" I called out from the platform, "Judy Bickle, come down here!"

Disoriented momentarily, she felt her heart beat faster. Then without thinking, she instinctively stepped into the aisle and made her way down front, where I stood waiting.

As Judy approached, I informed the congregation of her husband's situation, and a swell of prayers began to rise throughout the church. Likewise, I raised my voice in prayer, speaking words of faith for Craig's immediate healing.

Then suddenly, the spirit spoke to me. And placing my hand over the microphone, I leaned down to Judy's ear and whispered, "Have you and Craig been wanting children?"

I could see the surprise and confusion in her eyes. But after a moment, she wrinkled her brow and slowly nodded, "Yes".

Then out of nowhere, I again felt the spirit's leading. Raising the microphone, I heard my voice blare over the sanctuary's speakers. "You are going to conceive!"

As my words echoed throughout the building, Judy's mind raced. *"My husband is lying at death's door...and I-I-I'm gonna have a b-b-baby!?"*

Though I was surprised by my statement, I could see that she was stunned.

"I'm sorry," I recalled whispering in her direction, "I can't believe I'm telling you this." Yet before I could even inhale my next breath, I raised the microphone once again and declared, "By the way, it will be a girl."

As the crowded church erupted in praise, I felt a wave of prophetic words begin to flow, "She will be a mighty warrior for God...Many will be her fruits... and many will eat of her fruits... Even the world will be amazed at the things she will do..."

In that instant, Judy Bickle conceived the notion of *faith*. Listening to those words spoken with conviction, she no longer struggled to believe. Although Craig lay in a bed fighting for breath, she clung to what she had heard, and *believed* that they were *words of Life* -- sent directly to her and Craig from the Throne of God.

"It was like a gift of faith." She remembers: "I just received it as mine. I didn't care how or when, just that it was *going* to happen!"

Later that evening, smiling Judy Bickle sat on her husband's bed and lovingly announced, "I went to church tonight. Pastor Parsley prayed for you. And guess what? God told him and me and everyone in the church that *we* are going to have a baby!"

Looking up from his pillow, Craig simply drew in a breath and grinned...

Eight months later, everyone was breathing easier - especially Craig Bickle. Accomplishing what the doctors said could not be done, he was now 100% fully recovered and back to work.

The couple's simple belief in God's healing Word conceived the notion of Craig's complete recovery. Their choice to listen to God, rather than to the roaring waves of man's temporal facts, set in motion events that renewed their lease on life.

Coming home from work one afternoon, Craig entered the house, tossed his keys on the counter and called out to his wife: "Judy, I'm home." But his only answer was the 'r-r-ring' of the telephone. It was the doctor's office.

"Is this the Bickle residence?"

"Yes", Craig replied, controlling his apprehension.

"We just received the test results," the stoic voice on the other end began, "the doctor thought it best that you should know right away..."

Sitting down, Bickle gripped the receiver tightly in his hand.

"According to our findings, it looks like you are going...to have a baby!"

Before the last syllable was even spoken, Craig's lungs filled to capacity and he let out a "whoopie!" that yanked him straight out of his chair.

This time, the doctor's facts harmonized with God's eternal, healing truth. And in no time, a chaotic parade of family and friends showered them with gifts for their new addition.

"God turned it all around", Craig remembers. He healed me! And what God has done for us, surely He will do for all who will call on His name!"

Whatever you need: hope, help, healing, or even the patter of little feet around the house, if you put your trust in God's Words of Life and believe, ANYTHING you need - can be conceived.

FAITH COMETH BY...READING

Right now, specific parts of your body may be in so much pain that you would like to throw *them* over the side of a boat and be done with it, but that kind of attitude will only make your discomfort worse. You've got to stop focusing on the physical, and begin centering your attention on the spiritual. You'll never walk on the waves if you're sinking in despair.

To build up your faith to the level that the Bickles displayed, you have to do what Peter and the rest of the disciples did: walk and talk with Jesus on a daily basis.

In our modern world, such a thing can *still* be accomplished - and no complicated ritual of man or religion is necessary. By simply applying the power of God's Word through consistent study and prayer, you can have the kind of personal, one-on-one relationship with The Creator that was originally intended back in Eden's Garden.

In a mutual relationship, both parties get to know one another. God already knows you. He knew you before you were even born. And by studying the holy scriptures, you, in turn, can learn about Him and what He is capable of doing on your behalf. Through that consistent mind-renewing process, your expectation expands.

The more you know, the more faith grows. Diligent study of the scriptures re-programs your brain to the principles of God. It fine tunes your spirit to His holy will.

> *This book of the law shall not depart*
> *out of thy mouth: but thou shalt meditate*
> *therein day and night, that thou mayest*
> *observe to do according to all that is*
> *written therein: for then thou shalt make*
> *thy way prosperous, and then thou shalt*
> *have good success.*
>
> *(Joshua 1:8)*

Meditating "therein day and night" is simply storing up the Word of God in your spirit. It is opening the Bible and learning the 7,000-plus promises which God has put there "in writing" just for you. It is consistently applying those promises to your condition, day and night.

Learning the Godly guarantees which deal with your situation and rehearsing them over in your spirit will help you, like Peter, to possess the kind of faith that makes the impossible an everyday occurrence.

...thy faith hath made thee whole...
(Matthew 9:22)
Then touched He their eyes, saying,
According to your faith be it unto you.
And their eyes were opened...
(Matthew 9:29-30)
And all things, whatsoever ye shall
ask in prayer, believing, ye shall receive.
(Matthew 21:22)
If ye abide in Me, and My words
abide in you, ye shall ask what ye will,
and it shall be done for you.
(John 15:7)

Get a Word from God -- *and stick with it.* Even if you have to paper your walls with little yellow "stick'em" notes, keep His Words of faith and healing always before you.

...Incline thine ear unto my
sayings...for they are life...and health.
(Proverbs 4:20)

God's truth-filled Word will always outlive your circumstances, because The Word, like God Himself, never changes. The Apostle John put it best:

In the beginning was the Word, and the Word was with God, and the Word was God. The same was in the beginning with God. All things were made by Him; and without Him was not any thing made that was made.

(John 1:1-3)

In the beginning, He *spoke the Word*, and out of the nothingness of space, there was suddenly - Life! Using just His *Word*, God invented the sun, the moon, and endless galaxies of stars. But when it came to the creation of man, The Lord lovingly formed us with His Own hands.

He fashioned us using a rare combination of earthly flesh, a soul of free will, and a priceless eternal spirit ''tuned'' to Him.

This loving God, Who never changes, cared for us so much that when we freely chose to fall into Satan's contaminated clutch, He didn't dust us off His hands and try again; He declared war and put into motion a purification plan.

Reading His *Word*, it is obvious that God took upon Himself ''the hard part'' and willingly sacrificed His Own Son, so that through Christ's immunized blood, we are forgiven, purified, and able to choose again.

Here today, on the back side of Calvary, Satan's authority is broken. The serpent's puny arsenal of sickness is now nothing but a pesky fly, which we can easily swat - if we would simply choose to believe.

Like Christ in the garden of Gethsemane, we must stop focusing on the physical and turn our attention to the spirit of God within us. Doing so, we can easily overcome Satan's smoke screen of disease and selfish desire. All it takes is faith - an unwavering expectation in the promises of God's Word.

If through the "filter" of the old blood covenant the Lord was able to declare, *"I am the God that healeth thee"*, then here on the back side of Calvary, through the immunized blood of His Son, how much better for us is God's healing Word?

If the Lord and His Word never change, and if He created life with a spoken thought, then He is *still* able to speak into existence whatever you need today.

Healing is not hard. It is as simple and easy as saying, "I believe Your Word, Lord. Now speak. Create new life in me."

. . . .

GOD'S WORD ON HEALING

TO RECEIVE HEALING, SIN MUST BE CLEANSED

If my people, which are called by my name, shall humble themselves, and pray, and seek my face, and turn from their wicked ways; then will I hear from heaven, and will forgive their sin, and will heal their land.

(2 Chr 7:14)

I said, LORD, be merciful unto me: heal my soul; for I have sinned against thee.

(Psalms 41:4)

I have seen his ways, and will heal him: I will lead him also, and restore comforts unto him and to his mourners.

(Isaiah 57:18)

Then shall thy light break forth as the morning, and thine health shall spring forth speedily: and thy righteousness shall go before thee; the glory of the LORD shall be thy reward.

(Isaiah 58:8)

Return, ye backsliding children, and I will heal your backslidings. Behold, we

come unto thee; for thou art the LORD
our God.

(Jer 3:22)

Heal me, O LORD, and I shall be
healed; save me, and I shall be saved:
for thou art my praise.

(Jer 17:14)

For I will restore health unto thee,
and I will heal thee of thy wounds, saith
the LORD; because they called thee an
Outcast, saying, This is Zion, whom no
man seeketh after.

(Jer 30:17)

Behold, I will bring it health and
cure, and I will cure them, and will reveal
unto them the abundance of peace and
truth.

(Jer 33:6)

Come, and let us return unto the
LORD: for he hath torn, and he will heal
us; he hath smitten, and he will bind us
up.

(Hosea 6:1)

I will heal their backsliding, I will
love them freely: for mine anger is turned
away from him.

(Hosea 14:4)

O LORD my God, I cried unto thee,
and thou hast healed me.

(Psalms 30:2)

Why art thou cast down, O my soul? and why art thou disquieted within me? hope thou in God: for I shall yet praise him, who is the health of my countenance, and my God.

(Psalms 42:11)

He healeth the broken in heart, and bindeth up their wounds.

(Psalms 147:3)

A wicked messenger falleth into mischief: but a faithful ambassador is health.

(Prov 13:17)

The centurion answered and said, Lord, I am not worthy that thou shouldest come under my roof: but speak the word only, and my servant shall be healed.

(Matt 8:8)

And make straight paths for your feet, lest that which is lame be turned out of the way; but let it rather be healed.

(Heb 12:13)

Confess your faults one to another, and pray one for another, that ye may be healed. The effectual fervent prayer of a righteous man availeth much.

(James 5:16)

Beloved, I wish above all things that thou mayest prosper and be in health, even as thy soul prospereth.

(3 John 1:2)

Who forgiveth all thine iniquities; who healeth all thy diseases;

(Psalms 103:3)

FAITH BRINGS HEALING

And when he heard of Jesus, he sent unto him the elders of the Jews, beseeching him that he would come and heal his servant.

(Luke 7:3)

For she said within herself, If I may but touch his garment, I shall be whole. But Jesus turned him about, and when he saw her, he said, Daughter, be of good comfort; thy faith hath made thee whole. And the woman was made whole from that hour.

(Matt 9:21,22)

And when Jesus departed thence, two blind men followed him, crying, and saying, Thou Son of David, have mercy on us. And when he was come into the house, the blind men came to him: and

Jesus saith unto them, Believe ye that I am able to do this? They said unto him, Yea, Lord. Then touched he their eyes, saying, According to your faith be it unto you. And their eyes were opened; and Jesus straitly charged them, saying, See that no man know it.

(Matt 9:27-30)

While he spake these things unto them, behold, there came a certain ruler, and worshipped him, saying, My daughter is even now dead: but come and lay thy hand upon her, and she shall live.

(Matt 9:18)

And when Jesus came into the ruler's house, and saw the minstrels and the people making a noise, He said unto them, Give place: for the maid is not dead, but sleepeth. And they laughed him to scorn. But when the people were put forth, he went in, and took her by the hand, and the maid arose.

(Matt 9:23-25)

HIS WORD ISSUES HEALING

He sent his word, and healed them, and delivered them from their destructions.
(Psalms 107:20)

And he sent them to preach the kingdom of God, and to heal the sick.
(Luke 9:2)
And they departed, and went through the towns, preaching the gospel, and healing every where.
(Luke 9:6)
And the people, when they knew it, followed him: and he received them, and spake unto them of the kingdom of God, and healed them that had need of healing.
(Luke 9:11)
And Jesus said unto the centurion, Go thy way; and as thou hast believed, so be it done unto thee. And his servant was healed in the selfsame hour.
(Matt 8:13)
Wherefore neither thought I myself worthy to come unto thee: but say in a word, and my servant shall be healed.
(Luke 7:7)

JESUS CHRIST IS
HEALING PERSONIFIED

But he was wounded for our transgressions, he was bruised for our iniquities: the chastisement of our peace

*was upon him; and with his stripes we
are healed.*

(Isaiah 53:5)
*And Jesus saith unto him, I will come
and heal him.*

(Matt 8:7)
*And when he had called unto him
his twelve disciples, he gave them power
against unclean spirits, to cast them out,
and to heal all manner of sickness and all
manner of disease.*

(Matt 10:1)
*Came behind him, and touched the
border of his garment: and immediately
her issue of blood stanched.*

(Luke 8:44)
*And Jesus went forth, and saw a
great multitude, and was moved with
compassion toward them, and he healed
their sick.*

(Matt 14:14)
*And great multitudes came unto him,
having with them those that were lame,
blind, dumb, maimed, and many others,
and cast them down at Jesus' feet; and he
healed them:*

(Matt 15:30)

Heal the sick, cleanse the lepers, raise the dead, cast out devils: freely ye have received, freely give.
(Matt 10:8)

And he healed many that were sick of divers diseases, and cast out many devils; and suffered not the devils to speak, because they knew him.
(Mark 1:34)

And they that were vexed with unclean spirits: and they were healed.
(Luke 6:18)

They also which saw it told them by what means he that was possessed of the devils was healed.
(Luke 8:36)

For unclean spirits, crying with loud voice, came out of many that were possessed with them: and many taken with palsies, and that were lame, were healed.
(Acts 8:7)

And as the lame man which was healed held Peter and John, all the people ran together unto them in the porch that is called Solomon's, greatly wondering.
(Acts 3:11)

And beholding the man which was healed standing with them, they could say nothing against it.

(Acts 4:14)

There came also a multitude out of the cities round about unto Jerusalem, bringing sick folks, and them which were vexed with unclean spirits: and they were healed every one.

(Acts 5:16)

And it came to pass, that the father of Publius lay sick of a fever and of a bloody flux: to whom Paul entered in, and prayed, and laid his hands on him, and healed him.

(Acts 28:8)

Who his own self bare our sins in his own body on the tree, that we, being dead to sins, should live unto righteousness: by whose stripes ye were healed.

(1 Pet 2:24)

How God anointed Jesus of Nazareth with the Holy Ghost and with power: who went about doing good, and healing all that were oppressed of the devil; for God was with him.

(Acts 10:38)

HEALING IS FOR EVERYONE

*And great multitudes followed him;
and he healed them there.*

(Matt 19:2)

*For he had healed many; insomuch
that they pressed upon him for to touch
him, as many as had plagues.*

(Mark 3:10)

*And straightway the fountain of her
blood was dried up; and she felt in her
body that she was healed of that plague.*

(Mark 5:29)

*Now when the sun was setting, all
they that had any sick with divers diseases
brought them unto him; and he laid his
hands on every one of them, and healed
them.*

(Luke 4:40)

*And the whole multitude sought to
touch him: for there went virtue out of
him, and healed them all.*

(Luke 6:19)

THE RESULT OF HEALING IS PRAISE

*And one of them, when he saw that
he was healed, turned back, and with a
loud voice glorified God...*

(Luke 17:15)

Now Peter and John went up together into the temple at the hour of prayer, being the ninth hour. And a certain man lame from his mother's womb was carried, whom they laid daily at the gate of the temple which is called Beautiful, to ask alms of them that entered into the temple; Who seeing Peter and John about to go into the temple asked an alms. And Peter, fastening his eyes upon him with John, said, Look on us. And he gave heed unto them, expecting to receive something of them.

Then Peter said, Silver and gold have I none; but such as I have give I thee: In the name of Jesus Christ of Nazareth rise up and walk. And he took him by the right hand, and lifted him up: and immediately his feet and ancle bones received strength. And he leaping up stood, and walked, and entered with them into the temple, walking, and leaping, and praising God.

(Acts 3:1-8)

And it came to pass on a certain day, as he was teaching, that there were Pharisees and doctors of the law sitting by, which were come out of every town of Galilee, and Judaea, and Jerusalem: and the power of the Lord was present to heal them.

And, behold, men brought in a bed a man which was taken with a palsy: and they sought means to bring him in, and to lay him before him. And when they could not find by what way they might bring him in because of the multitude, they went upon the housetop, and let him down through the tiling with his couch into the midst before Jesus.

And when he saw their faith, he said unto him, Man, thy sins are forgiven thee. And the scribes and the Pharisees began to reason, saying, Who is this which speaketh blasphemies? Who can forgive sins, but God alone?

But when Jesus perceived their thoughts, he answering said unto them, What reason ye in your hearts? Whether is easier, to say, Thy sins be forgiven thee; or to say, Rise up and walk? But that ye may know that the Son of man hath power upon earth to forgive sins, (he said unto the sick of the palsy,) I say unto thee, Arise, and take up thy couch, and go into thine house. And immediately he rose up before them, and took up that whereon he lay, and departed to his own house, glorifying God.

(Luke 5:17-25)

And he was teaching in one of the synagogues on the sabbath. And, behold, there was a woman which had a spirit of infirmity eighteen years, and was bowed together, and could in no wise lift up herself. And when Jesus saw her, he called her to him, and said unto her, Woman, thou art loosed from thine infirmity. And he laid his hands on her: and immediately she was made straight, and glorified God.

(Luke 13:10-13)

And one of them, when he saw that he was healed, turned back, and with a loud voice glorified God, And fell down on his face at his feet, giving him thanks: and he was a Samaritan.

(Luke 17:15-16)

And Jesus said unto him, Receive thy sight: thy faith hath saved thee. And immediately he received his sight, and followed him, glorifying God: and all the people, when they saw it, gave praise unto God.

(Luke 18:42-43)

Rod Parsley began his ministry as an energetic 21-year-old in the backyard of his parent's Ohio home. The fresh, "old-time gospel" approach of Parsley's delivery immediately attracted a hungry, God-seeking audience. From the 17 people who attended that first 1977 backyard meeting, the crowds grew rapidly.

Today, as the pastor of Columbus, Ohio's 5,200 seat World Harvest Church, Parsley oversees World Harvest's K-12 Christian Academy; a growing Bible Institute; and numerous church sponsored outreaches including *"Lifeline,"* a pro-life organization, *"Lightline,"* an anti-pornography league, and *"Breakthrough,"* World Harvest Church's daily and weekly television broadcast, currently on 160 stations and three satellite networks across America.

Pastor Rod Parsley also serves as Dr. Lester Sumrall's personal assistant in directing the End-Time "Feed The Hungry" program.

To contact Rod Parsley,
write:

World Harvest Church
P. O. Box 32932
Columbus, Ohio 43232

*Please include your prayer requests
and comments when you write.*

Additional copies of this book
are available from you local bookstore
or from:

Harrison House
P. O. Box 35035
Tulsa, Oklahoma 74153

For additional copies
of this book
in Canada contact:

Word Alive
P. O. Box 284
Niverville, Manitoba
CANADA R0A 1E0

For international sales in Europe,
contact:

Harrison House Europe
Belruptstrasse 42 A
A - 6900 Bregenz
AUSTRIA

The Harrison House Vision

Proclaiming the truth and power
Of the Gospel of Jesus Christ
With excellence;

Challenging Christians to
Live victoriously,
Grow spiritually,
Know God intimately.